# INSPIRED
# LIVING

I0086716

# THE INSPIRATION
# AND WRITING OF
# *"THE CALLING"*

# BY ROBIN GODFREY

# INSPIRED LIVING

Copyright © 2015 Robin Godfrey

Printed in the United States of America

**ISBN-13:978-0692607367**
**ISBN-10:0692607366**

Printed by Createspace 2015
Published by BlaqRayn Publishing Plus 2015

# DEDICATION

*This writing is dedicated to my Lord and Savior, Jesus. It is also dedicated to my sister, Sylvia Godfrey, who was with me from the beginning of the writing of my first book and throughout the project. Sylvia, your knowledge, wisdom, understanding, and steadfast spirit amazes me.*

*Thank you for allowing God to use you in such a powerful way in my life and ministry. May God continue to mold you as He uses your gifts for His glory and may His blessings touch every part of your life.*

*Blessings always!*

**INSPIRED LIVING**

**The Inspiration and Writing of**
**"*The Calling*"**

*James 2: 20 But wilt thou know,*
*O vain man, that faith without*
*works is dead?*
*2 Corinthians 5:7 For we walk by*
*faith, not by sight*

**Inspired Living** is a short inspirational writing that tells the whole story of how **The Calling** was inspired and written. It gives the step-by-step details of hearing from God and taking action. It is often the case that we are hearing God leading us, but we never experience the divine manifestation of His work, because we do not act on what He is telling us. I pray that through reading this testimony of the move of God, you will be propelled to allow The Lord to work through you, today. As you grow in your walk with God, refer often to the two scriptures listed above to help you to move self out of the way and let God have His way. Hallelujah!

*The Calling* is a book that serves primarily three distinct purposes, which are each presented differently in the writing. The obvious, generalized purpose of the book appears on the front cover,' *A Guide to Help You Discover Your Divine Calling.* As the reader begins to travel through the chapters, he discovers that there is much more to the book than just discovering one's calling. In fact, it addresses the three-fold mission of a believer in Christ. One is that believers are called to seek the lost and lead them to salvation (*Matthew 28: 19-20*). Another is the call for every believer to edify (mature, enlighten, build up) the body of Christ (*1 Corinthians 14: 12, 26)*. Still another is that each believer is called to self edify (to learn, grow, change, mature) in Christ (*Romans 12: 2)*.   My assignment was clear, and it was to get the invitation to salvation out to as many people as the book could reach. Extend the invitation far beyond the walls of the local church. Get it into homes, places of employment, grocery stores, and anywhere else that God would take the book. If those who are already saved could re-focus on the missions, as stated in the Word and believe the Word which proclaims that God does speak to His sheep, then the body would be edified, motivated, and energized to get the invitation to salvation out to all who would accept Christ.

**The Calling** begins by telling

briefly about the Saturday morning when I first began to write the book and it ends by confessing that God told me to write long before the morning I started to write this particular book. It doesn't go into much about how the book was written, as it was about the three divine missions listed above, while also focusing on the need for each of us to learn to hear from God and accept His calling on our lives. The story of how the book came together; however, is a testimony, in itself, about hearing from God and doing what He says.  What I experienced in writing this book shows what happens when we seek to hear Jesus, before we go forth to work for Him on an assignment. Now, this writing is being presented, as a tool to win souls, also. It tells how the book was written and how chapter 9 came to be dedicated to the three survivors of the tragedy at Emanuel AME church, who were in the Bible Study class.

**<u>The Calling</u>** reveals that at the time I woke up and the Spirit told me to begin to write this work of inspiration, He was very specific and urgent. He said, "I want you to write and write right now. Tell everyone that they must be born again, how to be born again and how to hear me and obey what I say." This was not an audible voice, but hearing God speak to me clearly from within. Well, I sat up and immediately started to question God. I said something to this effect. "What are you talking about, Lord? I don't even have a computer anymore. You know that I no longer work from home, and I do not have a computer available to use for this. I have given away every computer I owned. I don't have any money to buy anything right now. What am I supposed to do?" He kept pressing and did not let up. "You need to write down what I give you and you also need to get a computer now. Get it now and write what I am giving you, now."

I got up, got my pad, pen, and Bible. I started to pray, as I walked around gathering myself and my things and then I started to write. I turned the first page of the pad I had chosen and what I saw was the sermon, ***Something is Calling Me to Get Back in the Saddle Again***. It is the story of the calling and anointing of David. And the Spirit said, write it and get it in your spirit again. Now, as my normal reaction is, I began to speak to the Lord again. I told Him that I had already written that sermon and, in fact, had already preached it. I asked Him why I needed to write it again. And this time, He explained very clearly. I told you to preach for Me, but you knew when you accepted My call that I also told you to write for me and to inspire My people for Me, so you have not fulfilled My total call for service. The reason you must also write it down in the form of a book is because people will not only hear The Word, as you preach it, but they will also have it to go back to again and again, as often as they need it. They will search the scriptures over and over and I will use The Word that I send through you to bring thousands of people to Myself. So, you need to read this message again, and this time, get the point. And when I read the sermon that morning, I got it. He was telling me to *Get Back in the Saddle Again*.

He showed me how we all wrestle with our purpose and we all forget over and over again why we were called to the specific work we are doing. We all need the constant reminder that we are on the battlefield for Our Lord, and not for ourselves. God has not changed His plans for the salvation of His people, and it will be fulfilled by our obedience to

Him.    I began by reading that sermon again, and then I started to write the Foreword and then the dedication, which opens the book. The foreword speaks of humanity's quest for understanding God and what He is calling each of us to do and to be. The dedication initially only consisted of the part that dedicated the work to The Lord and to His people. The specific dedication to the survivors came later, after the book was completely written. You will read about that later in this writing.

So, I opened the first chapter by writing what was happening, on that particular Saturday morning. And whatever the Lord told me, I kept right on writing. Hours passed without my realizing it. When I got to the point that the Lord told me to insert the sermon, The Spirit said, "I told you to get a computer. You are going to need to have a computer going forward. You are not going to be able to write an entire book and then go back and type it later, when you decide to get a computer. Now, go get a computer." This was when I realized that it wasn't going to just be a short writing, but it was to be a whole book. So, I know you all have gotten my pattern by now. I started speaking to the Lord again. I told Him how much money I had in my savings account and that He knew what it was being saved for. It was not for the purchase of a computer. I didn't have enough available funds for me to just go out and get a nice computer. I told Him that He knew what kind of computer I really wanted and that is why I don't have one right now. I told Him that I want a computer with a great big screen, because my vision is not what it used to be when I was younger. I want a huge screen so that I can have several applications open at the same time and I want the font to be large enough for me to work with everything unhindered. And I can't function with less than what I need to work with. I told Him how I was tired of struggling to do His work. Note, I wasn't being disrespectful to God at all. I was being honest with Him, because I truly believe that He is the only one who really really knows exactly how I feel and everything that I had been through in my life. The whole time that I was pouring out to God what I had to say, He kept saying, "I've got you.   I've got you. Go get it. Get it and do what I am telling you. I've got you." I could hear Him, like a drum roll while I was talking to Him … and I kept right on talking. I told The Lord that I was tired and fed up with seeing His people fighting from within the body just to be free to work for Him and I was tired too.    I thought the fight was supposed to be against the devil and not against each other. I don't feel like having to defend myself and the fact that I really do believe His Word that tells us that in Him, we are free to love everybody, even people who don't love us back. I said, "I'm tired, Lord, and I really don't feel like putting myself out there, where people can beat me down with mean spirited comments and actions. I am tired of hurting while I love. In fact, to love people like You have made me love people, really hurts and to be honest, Lord, I am tired." He just kept saying, "I know. I've got you. I love you. I will support you if nobody else does. Get the computer, Robin, and I will write through you. I will heal you and I will heal others also. Remember, hurting people hurt people. Don't worry, I will heal others who are around you. I need to use you right now. I want you to write down what I give you and get it out there. Tell My people how I love them. Tell them how to hear My voice. Tell them how to grow in Christ and thousands will be saved, set free, and delivered. I have been patient with you, but you need to get up and go get the computer." Now, in the interest of honesty, please understand that I may not have written everything He said in exact order, because of my memory, but what you just read is exactly what He said to me.

Then He said something new and challenging for me. He said, "Keep your mouth closed and let your actions speak. You don't need to explain yourself to anyone. You just need to obey Me." And I knew what He meant, so I ran to Sylvia (my sister who would become my editor), and I said,

"Sylvia, I have to get a computer and I have to get it now. God told me to get a computer and to write and I don't have any money for this right now. I don't know what to do, but I have to get a computer right now." She told me to calm down and she said, "Explain to me what is going on". So I began to tell her what was happening. I gave her what I had already written, the foreword and dedication and the beginning of the first chapter. While she was reading, I was getting washed up and ready to go. To make this long story short, I spent the remainder of that day, working on getting the computer. By the next day, I had the computer with the huge screen, the cordless keyboard and mouse and the printer. My brother, Ellis, our family's audio/visual expert, set it all up for me. And the rest is history.

Fast forward through the writing. God gave me chapter 1 first, then he continued over the months by giving me chapter 2, followed by chapter 3. He gave me chapters 4, 5, 6, 7 and chapter 8, in that order and I wrote exactly what He told me. Sylvia edited every chapter I wrote, as I completed each. Every Saturday, at brunch, I would read my latest writing to my mother and sister. I continued to go about my daily life, but God would get me up early in the morning and He would lead me through His Word. He would have me up late at night sometimes in His Word and directing me through the writing. After two chapters, I faltered and mentioned to two other people that I was writing a book. Jesus corrected me quite well and reminded me to close my mouth, stay in the Word, pray and write. Only discuss this with the people He placed in my life to make it happen. He said that the work will speak for itself when He releases it, and He would tell me how and when to do so. Until then, be quite. I closed my mouth and worked.

When I completed chapter 8, The Lord went silent for a time and I told Sylvia that I think the book is coming to an end, but the Lord says that I will be writing on a continual basis. I told her that I was waiting for chapter 9, but hadn't gotten anything from Him yet.

During these rare down-times, I would go back into the chapters I had written and make the corrections that the editor had sighted. Then late one night, God said, "Chapter 10 will be the last chapter and it will be ***Work for*** *__the Night Is Coming__*.    So I said, "OK, Lord, but I need chapter 9 right now, please." He said, "Read the sermon, *__Work for the Night is Coming__* and begin to type it in." Well, I said, "OK, Lord, but I am waiting for chapter 9 right now. What are You doing?" I got no answer. So I read the sermon and began to type chapter 10. Midway through this writing, He says, "Begin chapter 9 with the names and ages of the Emanuel 9. \When I had done that, He told me to write the names of the news reporter and cameraman who were murdered in Virginia on live TV." So I did it and He began to give me a Word for chapter 9. He was moving much faster than I was and He was giving me the *Closing Word*, as well, and I found myself going back and forth between the three different writings and suddenly, the book came to an end.

I was finished, so I began to finalize the structure of the book, to include writing the page *About the Author*, the *Content Page*, and the *Title Page*. Now, at this point, I was waiting to hear from God concerning when He wanted me to move forward with contacting the publisher He had chosen for this book. There was silence. Time kept passing and I was hearing nothing from God that propelled me to move forward in having the work published, so I went on with my life. Then it happened again. I woke up early on a Saturday morning with the Lord telling me to write chapter 1 of my second book. Well, I wasn't expecting this so I began as usual to question God. "What do you mean, write? You haven't done anything with the first book yet. Why should I keep writing when You aren't saying anything about **The Calling**? I'm not settled in my Spirit. I don't know what to do." He said, "Write what I tell you." And I went to the computer and started writing, **In the Morning When I Rise**, chapter 1 of book 2. I was crying and complaining as I wrote chapter 2, **Fear is not Faith**. But I found that this book I was writing was exciting. It is completely different from **The Calling**. It has a different flow, a different feel, a different message, but the same call to salvation, repentance, and service. It is, as my Aunt Rebecca described **The Calling**, delicious!

Oh yes, back to **The Calling.** I was left wondering why I wasn't told to send it to the publisher. So let us visit that part of my assignment,   because it tells how

## INSPIRED LIVING

He orchestrates His work. I was asked to assist in the hiring process at work and I interviewed candidates who applied. Two beautiful ladies were hired. As I was going through this process of writing, one of the two came into the office with a book of poetry she had written. The cover, artistry and format was breathtaking! For weeks I just kept writing my book and at work I was helping to train both recent hires, but I didn't say that I was writing a book. I asked the poet if it was difficult for her to get her book published and if it was expensive. She freely explained the process to me and answered my countless questions. I inquired of the publisher she used and she spoke highly of her experience with **BlaqRayn Publishing** in North Carolina. She provided the contact information to me and told the publisher about me, after I shared with her what I had been working on. I researched other publishers, before I spoke with my co-worker, because while writing at home, advertisements for publishing books kept popping up while I was searching scriptures. I read many reviews from other writers and found that God was not leading me to publish and market this work through any of the publishers I read about.

From the beginning of this
assignment and throughout the
project, I never had to deviate
from my normal routine to go out
and seek guidance. He kept
bringing what I needed to me.
God chose ***BlaqRayn Publishing***
and brought them to me at work.
When I finally contacted this
publishing company, they literally
walked me through the entire
process. God also paid for the
book before it was completed.
He was proving to me that I do
not have to go out and network.
I do not have to compromise the
truth of His Word, in order to

reach a larger audience or for Him to be accepted. I need only to obey Him and He will lead me through what He has called me to do. He never told me to go and make it happen. He said, *My sheep hear My voice and follow me*. Through this work He was teaching me how to follow. But the work was still in my computer, not yet published, I was working on a second book, and He had already told me about writing **Inspired Living**, so I knew I had some more listening to do. I had a whole lot going on, but nothing was completed.

The night of Friday, September 11,

# INSPIRED LIVING

2015, my sister brought a News and Courier article to me concerning the Emanuel tragedy, and said, "Mama said you have to read this one. It's about the survivors of the Emanuel 9 tragedy" and she left the room. I started to read the article and when I got to the words that Ms. Sheppard said, I got excited, because I now had her name. I had been praying for them all the time, but I would always ask The Lord to bless the lady who the suspect said he didn't kill because he wanted her to tell the story of what happened in the church. I never knew her name. So I stopped reading and thanked God that I now had a name to pray for and I prayed for her right then and there. Then I went on to read what Mrs. Sanders had to say and I was talking aloud at the time saying, "I am praying for you all constantly. I've only reached out to you in the form of a sympathy card that Sylvia and I sent early on, but I never contacted you all directly." I placed my Amen to all that she had to say. Her words brought to mind what I had been saying to my family over the months following the tragedy.

I had spoken about all of the media attention and of the dignitaries from our local churches that were always before us. I kept wondering if any of these powerful figures were in contact with those who were in that room, who must be traumatized and struggling. I was wrestling in my heart with hearing about all of the money that was coming in and the flag coming down. I wrestled with hearing the politicians and media as they focused America's attention on our great state of South Carolina and how the tragedy brought out a love that I could not really relate to, while hurting inside. I kept saying that love would reach out to those hurting people who were in the church, in prayer. And I hoped that love was reaching out to make sure that their faith wasn't shattered to pieces. I hoped that this love I was seeing on TV was telling them that God did not sit silently on the sidelines while someone attempted to kill them and actually did kill people in front of them. Evil did what they experienced in that church! But love is speaking to all of us, loudly, in the midst of the tragedy. Love is saying, "Hold on to your faith! Cleave more closely to Him for the answers to all of the questions you must have." And that's when the Spirit said to me, "Now you get it! Stop looking at what others may not have done or may have done, because you can only look at the outside of any man. I look at the heart. Look instead at what you have done and what you have not done to reach out to them." And that's when He told me, "I want you to dedicate chapter 9 of the first book to the three survivors who were in My Bible Study. There is healing in chapter 9, not only for them, but for anyone who will read the book. Include them in the book."    Then He said, "Include the survivor of the shooting in Virginia, also, and Robin, get the book published. Get the published work in their hands. It is anointed with My purpose and it will win thousands to salvation. My Word will go forth and will not return to me void."

I had to go back and read chapter 9 of **The Calling,** right then. I added The Emanuel 12 and dedicated chapter 9, as instructed. When asked, He said, I am healing Mrs. Pinckney and Reverend Pinckney's children also, as well as all other family members who were impacted by the loss of life. I am also healing my land, which has been plagued with tragedies, but my healing comes in different ways, according to the need and My purpose for each life.

## INSPIRED LIVING

I went to bed the night of September 11th, without knowing the name of the survivor in Virginia. But when I woke up the next morning, she was on my television and I added her name. The final word I typed was her name, Vicki Gardner, page 159. And immediately The Lord said, "Now contact the publisher and get it done."

On September 12, 2015, I contacted the publisher and submitted the manuscript for review. At 11:30 PM, 9/12/2015, God said, "I wanted the manuscript submitted today because it is 9-12, the two numbers that survivor, Mrs. Sanders, has been researching the significance of, 9 and 12. Today is the day that the first person who doesn't know you, someone from another state, not directly touched by the tragedy, will begin to read what I wrote through you. This work will not be contained in the four walls of a church, nor in the state of South Carolina. It will begin it's journey by crossing the state line. Now, be still and see what I will do with My Word. My Word is anointed to heal, to save, to set My people free, and deliver My people from sin."

And thus ends the story of the inspiration and writing of **The**

# INSPIRED LIVING

**<u>Calling</u>**. This story showed me just how closely Jesus will walk with us and how clearly He will speak to us and lead us, if we let Him do the work through us.

Will there be one who is willing to trust Jesus as Lord and Savior? Is there one who knows that they need to have a relationship with the one and only Savior that will walk with you and talk with you and lead you all the way from earth to glory?   Is there one who hears that still small voice of God calling you to salvation this day? If so, read on, and let the Word of God lead you into everlasting life.

# INSPIRED LIVING

*2 Corinthians 5: 21* tells us, *For he hath made him to be sin for us, who knew no sin; that we might be made the righteousness of God in him.* *John 3: 3-7* Jesus tells Nicodemus, *You must be born again.* These verses give us insight into salvation. God sent His only begotten Son into this sinful world to take your sin and mine upon Himself and to die in order to pay our sin debt in full. When the debt was paid, God raised His Son, Jesus, from the dead. He gave Jesus all authority, that through belief in Him, you and I would be saved from eternal death. If you believe this, then *Romans 10: 9-11* tells you what action you must take to be born again. It says, ***That if thou shalt confess with thy mouth the Lord Jesus, and shalt believe in thine heart that God hath raised him from the dead, thou shalt be saved. For with the heart man believeth unto righteousness; and with the mouth confession is made unto salvation. For the scripture saith, Whosoever believeth on him shall not be ashamed.***

Now pray, and ask God to forgive you for every sin. It doesn't matter how awful you think your sin is; Jesus knows and He loves you all the same. Receive His forgiveness.

## INSPIRED LIVING

Ask Him to lead you every day of your life going forward, and He will. Get in His Word and hear Him reveal His will for your life, through His Spirit that has now entered you, through salvation. Ask God to lead you to a church that believes, teaches and obeys His Word. Never look to go back to your former life. Press forward in your new life, because you can't go forward looking back.

God loves you and so do I.

**A message from the Lord, by the pen of Minister Robin Godfrey Bunkem**

# *The End*

## *Stay Tuned for My Upcoming Release*

## *Here is a Sneak Preview of Chapter One*

# INSPIRED LIVING

## *<u>In the Morning When I Rise</u>*

### 2 Timothy 1:5-6

*"I am reminded of your sincere faith, which first lived in your grandmother Lois and in your mother Eunice and, I am persuaded, now lives in you also.*

*For this reason I remind you to fan into flame the gift of God, which is in you through the laying on of my hands..."*

There are so many character traits that we receive from our family, some that we gladly own and others we wish we didn't inherit. I am like most people. I have acknowledged the great things I received from my parents. I got my personality, love of the ocean, and some artistic skills from my daddy. I got my creativity in the arts, love of music, and quiet meditation habits from my mom. Notice how all of that was positive. I refuse to acknowledge anything negative, and there is a reason for it. I know that every negative thing that lies within a person, can be changed.

The changes are already done in the Spirit realm. The first step to bringing them into the natural is to believe the Word of God.

The second step is to get in the Word and allow God to change the way we think and live, through His Word. When we "catch the wave", we are on our way. This means that we press toward the mark and we refuse to look back.

Children often times do not recognize where their traits came from. I was no different. I remember, as a child, that many people would say that I had my father's personality. I was one who simply loved everyone. I had never met a person I just didn't like, from the time I met them. There was no-one that simply wasn't "my cup of tea", for no reason at all. A person would have to do something specific that caused me to choose to reject their friendship. In fact, I really couldn't understand or accept the idea that someone did not like me, when they didn't even know me.

I have found that the character traits I just described has served me very well in working for the Lord. I loved music, probably before I was born. I got this from my mother, who was the organist at our church for fifty-nine years.

So I was present at every choir rehearsal, every church service, and every time she sat at the piano in our home to practice. I was blessed as a very young child, with a powerful voice and the ability to remember all the lyrics to the songs I heard. So I sang my heart out!

What positive traits did you inherit from your parents or grandparents? How did they show up in your youth? How have they been developed in your adulthood? Have you surrendered those traits to God for His service?

Look at the scripture, found in *2 Timothy 1*. Paul says there was an unfeigned faith that he was persuaded was in Timothy, which dwelt first in Timothy's grandmother Lois, and then in his mother Eunice. We are going to look at what Paul does, because he recognized what was within Timothy. Recognize today, that God made no mistake in choosing who would parent His children. I certainly have seen it in my own life and in the lives of those around me.

My father was born on the fourth of July, and every year, on the morning of his birthday, he would head out on a deep-sea fishing trip, in celebration. He loved to fish, so any time that he had a little free time to relax, you would find him fishing on some dock in Charleston, South Carolina. He had many fishing spots, but one that all of the family readily recalls is The Battery, in the city. He would often take my brothers fishing with him, but he also took the entire family on The Battery on Sunday afternoons. I realized, as a young adult, that I was drawn to the water. Every chance I get, I still go to the water. Well, I found that whenever I want to hear from God, if I would sit on The Battery, or on Colonial Lake, or at Brittle Bank Park, all popular locations by the water in Charleston, I could hear the voice of God so clearly.

It is in these places and other water spots I frequent, that I've found that I feel the presence of My Lord, and He begins to reveal His Word to me. I realized that the love of the water was not simply a love I received from my father. He was by the water for a reason and now, so am I, for God's glory.

Many years ago, I decided to go on a cruise to the Bahamas. While on the cruise, I found that early in the morning, I would rise and ascend to the upper deck of the ship. I would gaze out at the vast ocean all around me, with no sight of distant shores, and I loved it. This reminded me that my very life is in His hand. I would pray, while alone on deck, enjoying the cool breeze on my face, before everyone got up and filled the ship with the busyness of enjoying their vacation. I could commune with God on that ship, where I felt His presence moving the water and the air. We need to surrender those traits in our lives, for The Lord to use them.


*2 Timothy 1: 6* Paul goes on to say that because he recognizes that same faith in Timothy that had existed in his grandmother and his mother, he would lay hands on Timothy and Timothy would receive the gift of God, and Timothy was to remember to stir up that gift of God during his ministry. What gifts are lying dormant inside of you that need to be stirred up? Are you tapping into the power of the Holy Ghost that is within you, to speak life into those traits that are inside of you, for the Lord's service? Get into the Word of the Lord, receive what He is saying to the body, and purpose in your heart to stir up every gift He has placed within you, to be used by Him for the purpose of His mission.

God has given all of us the command to win souls to the Kingdom. This is accomplished by God, through faith in Jesus, His only begotten Son. It is done, here in the world, through you and through me, as we surrender every gift and every trait to Jesus, for service.

My father went home to be with The Lord many years ago, while I was still in high school, but even now, when I enter my mother's home, I often hear the sweet songs of Zion. She is either playing the radio or a CD or she is playing her piano, and sometimes singing as well. There is a very powerful presence of the Lord's Spirit in her home. It is another place of refuge, where I can sit and hear the voice of God. He reveals much to me, right there at mama's house.

Most days, a whole sermon is preached at her house, because there is such a free flow of the Spirit within those walls. Now, as I sit and type what God gives me, I often have songs of praise playing in the background, drowning out other distractions that may divert my attention from the call on my life to write for The Lord.

I found from writing the first book, that I will go into prayer while writing, so it is necessary that I explain going forward, that prayers that are going forth in the middle of my typing will be in bold print.

*I speak life into every gift that is within you, in the name of Jesus. Bless your servant, my Lord, right now, that the gifts will be revealed and stirred up, for Your glory. I rebuke every device of the enemy to suppress what You have ordained, before this child was formed in his mother's womb. Lord, you knew who they would be and what they would do for Your Kingdom, and I declare that it is done, in Your name. Have your way, Oh Lord. Have your way in the lives of Your people. You have all power and all glory is Yours, My Master. I declare that it is done in accord with Your Word. I love you, My Lord. Stir it up, Oh God! Stir it up! Reveal, Oh Lord. Reveal and release, God. Have Your way. Have Your way, in Jesus' name. Amen.*

When the people of God tap into divine order, spiritual gifts, and super-natural power, it's morning in our lives. When morning comes in your life, then you rise. Rising is an act of faith. And we all have that power and even that command to walk within the authority God has given to us, as women and men of God. Just as Paul did with Timothy, we are called to stir up those gifts of God within the believer. Church, it is time for us to wake up, because it is time for us to get up early and on fire for service to The Lord. It is a privilege to be called into His service. He has poured so much into every one of us and it began long before we were born, and we ought to give Him thanks. There is more to saying thank-you, however, than just saying the words. Thank-you is an action statement. Say thank-you by living out the thank-you. *Luke 6: 46* says, *And why call ye me, Lord, Lord, and do not the things which I say?* It's more to this life with the Lord than simply the things that we say, it must be followed with the things that we do. And those things we do must line up with the Word of God. We must do what He says. He says, *In everything give thanks: for this is the will of God in Christ Jesus concerning you. 1 Thessalonians 5:18.* So, we give Him thanks for all things, for everything He so perfectly placed within us, for what He is doing within us and for what He is doing through us. We release every gift of The Spirit, for His glory. Can you say it with me? "In the morning, when I rise,   I will give thanks by living out the Word of

God in my life. In the morning, when I rise, I will give thanks by pressing forward in my calling. In the morning, when I rise, I will live thank-you by using my gifts for His glory." Now, say thank-you for those genetic traits, by releasing them to God for His service. And in the morning, when you rise, your walk should show your thanks.

It is something special when we take time to reminisce on those great things that make us who we are are people of character, vision, and determination. Researching our genealogy is trending in recent

years in American society also, as
people are seeking to discover
more about what made them who
they are today. Well, in addition to
those inherited traits of character,
and those that were taught to us
that served to help us in forming
our moral standards, there are also
those facts and beliefs that we
learned from parents and
grandparents concerning our
spiritually, like Timothy.

As you spend some time in
thought about where your traits
and beliefs originated, give thanks
for those who contributed to
leading you to Christ. The sermon
you will read in a moment speaks

about how we are commanded to teach future generations about what The Lord has done and who He has been in our lives. It also addresses what may happen to future generations, if we fail to pass the Truth on to them.

# INSPIRED LIVING

## <u>Fifteen Minutes on a Mountain Top</u>

*Judges 2:7-14 (New King James Version)*

*[7] So the people served the LORD all the days of Joshua, and all the days of the elders who outlived Joshua, who had seen all the great works of the LORD which He had done for Israel. [8] Now Joshua the son of Nun, the servant of the LORD, died when he was one hundred and ten years old. [9] And they buried him within the border of his inheritance at Timnath Heres, in*

*the mountains of Ephraim, on the north side of Mount Gaash.* [10] When all that generation had been gathered to their fathers, another generation arose after them who did not know the LORD nor the work which He had done for Israel.

[11] *Then the children of Israel did evil in the sight of the LORD, and served the Baals;* [12] *and they forsook the LORD God of their fathers, who had brought them out of the land of Egypt; and they followed other gods from among the gods of the people who were all around them, and they bowed down to them; and they provoked the LORD to anger.* [13] *They*

*forsook the LORD and served Baal and the Ashtoreths.[a] 14 And the anger of the LORD was hot against Israel. So He delivered them into the hands of plunderers who despoiled them; and He sold them into the hands of their enemies all around, so that they could no longer stand before their enemies.*

The focus of this section of scripture is the obedience and disobedience of the Israelites. Theirs is a history of repeated good behavior followed by repeated bad behavior, repentance, good behavior, then bad behavior. Then there is the opposite pattern of Our Lord: forgiving and leading the Israelites, communing with them, then His wrath coming upon them in response to their disobedience. There is a definite pattern following these scriptures.

The second chapter of Judges begins with an angel of the Lord coming to the Israelites, reminding them of the victory God had lead them to in delivering them from Egyptian captivity by the parting of the Red Sea. The angel reiterates a truth of who The Lord is, as it tells them that the Lord said, "I will never break My own covenant with you." He proclaims to the

Israelites that they were not supposed to have an allegiance with the people of the land where they were, but instead they were to have destroyed the idols of that land, but they did not hold to their end of the command and "Why?" So, in keeping with the pattern of behavior, when the angel of the Lord finished, the Israelites lifted their voices and wept.

So they repented again for their disobedience, and we picked up today's lesson with verse seven, where they are now serving the Lord faithfully.

Now let us examine what

happened in this lesson by comparing verse seven with verse ten. Verse 7 tells us clearly that, *the people served the LORD all the days of Joshua, and all the days of the elders who outlived Joshua, who had seen all the great works of the LORD which He had done for Israel.* But verse ten tells us *another generation arose after them who did not know the LORD nor the work which He had done for Israel.*

**Point one** today is, if today's generation fails to proclaim the Good News of our Lord and Savior and the work He has done, the future generation will not know the Lord nor the work He has done.

The question today for self examination is, If I had fifteen minutes on a mountain top, what would I proclaim and why? **Fifteen minutes on a Mountain Top**

*Deuteronomy 6:5-12 (New King James Version)*

*5 You shall love the LORD your God with all your heart, with all your soul, and with all your strength.*

*6 "And these words which I command you today shall be in*

*your heart. [7] You shall teach them diligently to your children, and shall talk of them when you sit in your house, when you walk by the way, when you lie down, and when you rise up. [8] You shall bind them as a sign on your hand, and they shall be as frontlets between your eyes. [9] You shall write them on the doorposts of your house and on your gates. [10] "So it shall be, when the LORD your God brings you into the land of which He swore to your fathers, to Abraham, Isaac, and Jacob, to give you large and beautiful cities which you did not build, [11] houses full of all good things, which you did not fill, hewn-out wells which you did not dig, vineyards and olive trees which you did not plant—when you have eaten and are full— [12] then beware, lest you forget the LORD who brought you out of the land of Egypt, from the house of bondage.*

Again, the question we are asking today for self examination is, If I had fifteen minutes on a mountain top, what would I proclaim and why? **Fifteen minutes on a mountain top.**

**Point two** is that everyone that is

born again, has their own fifteen minutes on a mountain top, and many of us have it daily.

I often recall saying, "The world may do whatever it wants with me, but before last shovel of dirt covers my body, if given one last breath, I will tell someone about my Lord and Savior." The reality is, however, that we don't have to wait until it is our last breath. We can tell somebody, anybody, every body that Jesus is Lord and that Jesus saves. We need to understand today that this is not just a command for preachers; indeed it is a command for us all.

## INSPIRED LIVING

When we look at what happened here between verse seven and ten of Judges chapter two, we have to ask ourselves, what did these people teach the coming generation between Joshua and all the elders who outlived Joshua, so that they now have a generation of Israelites who did not know the Lord, nor the work that He had done. I will now suggest to us that there was a whole lot of talking going on, and a whole lot of business going on, but obviously, based upon the Word, they failed to do what we were told to do in *Deuteronomy*. So let's look at why they didn't do it. This word suggests that the message had not been in the Israelites' hearts.

*Deuteronomy 6:6* says the Word had to be in their hearts. Before we are going to be able to teach the Word diligently to the next generation and speak about it when we sit in our homes and when we walk in the way, it first has to be implanted in our own hearts. *Deuteronomy* was not just talking to the preachers.

I know when we think of fifteen minutes on a mountain top, we think of a proclamation of the gospel, but Deuteronomy was not making this command just to the preacher, but to the believers as a whole. Every one of us has our fifteen minutes on a mountain top, and some of us do have it daily. The question is what are we doing with our fifteen minutes?

Let us use our spiritual wings of imagination and think on what our moment of proclamation would sound like. Just think, if what you were saying for just fifteen minutes were being broadcast simultaneously into every household, into every ipod, on every television, radio, computer, into every car, truck, van or other mode of transportation (you get the point), what would everyone hear? Would you be taking every opportunity to make sure that those who hear what you have to say hear about a risen Savior, who had to come into this sinful world, by way of birth through an innocent virgin named Mary. I'm suggesting now, that the former generation didn't tell the people about the Lord and look at what happened over and over again.

**<u>Third and final point</u>** is when real life hits the next generation, they are going to need to know who God is and we have a charge to keep, and that charge is to let them know, before it is a day and a day too late. There are numerous stories of truth found in the Word of God. Let us visit just a couple of them to seal point number three. *Daniel 3* tells us the story of the three Hebrew boys who refused to bow down and worship the gold image that Nebuchadnezzar had erected and they were thrown into a fiery furnace, but I want you to realize today that someone had told those Hebrew boys about the one and only true and living Savior and they were saved from the heat of fire. Someone had been true to the command given in *Deuteronomy*, because they knew who the Lord was and the wonderful works He had done, and that same God took the fire out of the furnace where they were concerned. **When our coming generation is dealing with their fiery furnace, will we have told them, during our fifteen minutes on a mountain top, about our Lord and Savior.** Saints of God, we have a charge to keep and a God to glorify. Glorify Him by feeding His sheep.

In closing, we must look at what happened to this generation of Israelites. *Judges 2: 11-14* explains that this generation then did evil in the sight of the Lord.

They served the idol gods and they forsook the true and living Lord. And the wrath of God came against them so that they were not able to stand against their enemies. The fact of the matter is, if we who are saved, take our every opportunity (and there are many) to proclaim everything that is wrong with each other, everything that we disagree with in the world, and in essence *e*verything else except the Good News of The Gospel, the next generation will know everything else, except God.

**Fifteen minutes on a mountain top**... Everyday, every

single day, we need to await that fifteen minutes that we can tell somebody about our Lord and invite some soul to come into the fold. It begins with accepting the Good News within our own hearts, then we can *teach it diligently to our children, speak about it when we sit in our homes and when we walk along the way*. Don't keep it to yourself. Jesus is the only way to salvation and every generation needs to know.

When you have read this Word of encouragement, go forth with expectation daily of having your fifteen minutes on a mountain top. It may even be today in your own home, but purpose in your heart to give God the glory, and do it, if only for your fifteen minutes.

**In the morning when I rise**, I will give thanks to My Lord for all that is within me, because of Him, then I will teach all of it to someone else, during my fifteen minutes.

# About the Author

Minister Robin Godfrey Bunkem is a woman of God who is not ashamed of the Gospel. She is a native of Charleston, South Carolina. She accepted salvation at the age of 10, and became a member of Calvary Baptist Church, in Charleston, at the age of 12.

Her life's joy has always been sharing the truth of the Word. Minister Bunkem accepted the call to the preaching ministry, preached her initial sermon in November of 2008, and became a licensed minister.

She continues to boldly deliver

## INSPIRED LIVING

God's Word, whenever there is an opportunity.

BOOKS BY ROBIN GODFREY:

## THE CALLING